Control The Weather

A Believer's Guide to Victory Over Turbulent Weather

Ilene G. Saidel

Dedication

I dedicate this book to my pastor, Creflo A. Dollar, and my spiritual grandfather, Kenneth Copeland. For through their love and teaching, I have developed a great understanding of the Word of God. I have been inspired during some of the toughest challenges of my life to continue in the Word and to put the Word of God as my final authority no matter what things look like.   In all your getting, get understanding...

Visit my website at www.ilenesaidel.com

Ilene G. Saidel

Contents

Introduction

I am a faith person, a believer, and I have been speaking to the deadliest of storms and turbulent weather for quite some time - and they have obeyed my commands, and continue to obey. Since God is not a respecter of persons, you can expect to do the same... Trust and be confident... Confident in His ability – and the authority given to you as a believer.

You are not powerless when turbulent weather threatens your home and family

Whether there's the threat of a (major) storm or you just have some special outdoor plans and rain is on the way, you can do something about it. With all of the horrific weather and storms and changeable weather patterns that have been plaguing the world for the past fifteen to twenty years, it can be comforting to know that you can do something about it.

Weather is something that we talk about and hear people complain about, and they think that nothing can be done about it except to talk or complain about it. Granted, it is sometimes something we talk about even with strangers or friends to break the ice or something that is a common ground for starting up a conversation.

I wrote this book to help lift your level of expectation for the supernatural and for walking in your authority on this earth. It's a passion of mine to see others walk it out and live supernaturally.

I have a passion for the supernatural – it is just not enough for me to live a natural life and I believe that God did not create you to live just like a natural man on this earth either. And, so, I have been speaking to weather and commanding it to obey me for over 15 years. After seeing these wonderful results (wow) I just cannot help but share with millions of people all over the world that they can control the weather and not be feeling powerless about it. As a born again believer*, you are called to do the works that Jesus did – and greater- after all, we do serve a supernatural God. Walking in the supernatural is what Jesus did – so we must be doers and not just hearers of the Word. And, it is the Father within you that does the work, not you. It is not your ability; it is His ability.

Jesus told us that we would do those works that He did (and greater) – in John 14:12 (New Living Translation) Jesus tells us that

> I tell you the truth, anyone who believes
> in me will do the same works I have done,
> and even greater works, because I am
> going to be with the Father.

One of those works that Jesus did was to calm the storms and declare peace over them. If you are in Christ - a born-again believer - than you have the authority to speak to storms – you have Jesus living on the inside of you – you are seated in heavenly places with Christ Jesus - and all things are under your feet since you are part of the Body of Christ (and all things are under the feet of Jesus). The same God Who spoke the world into existence lives in you. Need I say more?

Let me mention that there is no such person as Mother Nature. There is God the Father who is in control - however he created man to have dominion over His creation. Everything that God created is good and He expects man to manage His creation. Man is to manage God's creation since everything is God's and it all belongs to Him. And, since everything is God's and you are God's child, than it belongs to you. Without going into the account of the Garden of Eden and the Fall with Adam's Original Sin as it is called, this book is meant to describe how to walk in the authority over the weather. It is not my intent to coerce you into acting; you will need to hear and do and be a doer of the Word. There is probably significant reason to want to walk in that authority since turbulent weather is just about an everyday occurrence. And, I encourage you to go for it - believe and do - and you will see the results. Trust in the Lord with all your heart and lean not into your own understanding, your own reasoning, your own evaluation, your own analysis.

When God created man (God is the creator of all), He blessed man and gave man dominion:

> And God blessed them and told them, "Multiply and fill the earth and subdue it." (Gen 1:28).

God said men were to "be masters over all life." (Gen 1:26 NLT). As a born again believer God expects you to be just like His son Jesus. And, when Jesus encountered foul weather, what did He do? He spoke to it, not about it. When He spoke to the fig tree and told it what to do, He did not look back. He just turned and walked away expecting the results. Expecting the fig tree to obey Him.

Demonic Weather Patterns

I believe that there are foul weather spirits that do control out of whack weather or turbulent conditions, but we have dominion over them. It is not accidental nor is it from God when there are damaging storms such as tornadoes and hurricanes. It may be beyond the scope of this book to go into the what's and why's but I do believe that although God is sovereign, He is not always in control only because man has free will and authority. If you do not agree, just take a look at things that are "bad" in this world like murders for example – God does not cause murders but it is man who does those works via his free will. I believe that the buildup of sin in the earth is part of the reason that there are so many "bad" storms. Argue with me if you must... there is more in the "unseen" realm, the unseen world than you know. And, issues that appear in the seen realm have origin in the unseen realm, the unseen spiritual world.

Many times, I have prayed away storms and left home only to return to find out that there was some rain but no damage and it didn't even come near me, my home or the location where I traveled to. A thousand shall fall at my side....ten thousand at my right but it will not come near me. Nor will it come near you.

Do it Afraid

Am I ever "fearful" during bad weather? I must admit there were times when my life could have been in great jeopardy, and yes, I might have felt fear for a second when I thought what would happen if the weather did not obey "that time." But I went ahead and did what I knew to do. I did it "afraid." I always strive to do what God says to do although it might not make any sense. If you need to go and take cover after or before the prayer, you need to do the natural thing as well. Always be led by the Holy Spirit. Just because you pray – don't tempt those angels of yours even if *do* have divine protection. Do not be afraid to step out and miss it... practice on the rain... practice on believing for God to protect you even if you are walking along in broiling hot sunlight... He can put a cloud over you to protect you. Just believe.

The Norm for a Believer

From almost day one, when I got saved, I walked in the supernatural. I meditated in the Word of God - in particular John 14:12. Is speaking to the weather and seeing it change a miracle? I truly believe that God intended for His children, the believers, those who know who and whose they are, to walk in their authority on an everyday basis. I believe that when you speak to storms and they die down or leave your territory, that it is not so much a miracle but the manifestation of your authority. It is the answered prayer- we can call it if you would prefer. So, it may appear to be a miracle when it happens, but I believe that the supernatural is really the norm for a believer. Or, I should say, a "believer" who believes! Walking in the supernatural like Jesus did should be our norm.

What is Dominion and Why is it Important?

Dominion is simply defined as "dominance," "the right to rule over something." As a believer you have dominion over everything and every situation no matter what. And, seated with Christ in heavenly places, far above the "situation" - and it is under your feet. With God all things are possible so with you all things are possible. Dominion is part of your right and that is important, and with the spirit of the living God inside you, and being God-inside minded, you have the authority on this earth. You have the authority to be effective with God's ability. Remember, it's not your own ability, it is His ability. And, dominion is enforced by your words out of your mouth just like God Who created the world with His words. God said... and, God said.... And God saw.

Scriptures – You Have Dominion

There are scriptures that support your authority as a believer (after all, they are the truth) and your "ability" which is really Jesus' ability to speak to "mountains" or, in this case, storms or impending storms, and tell them where to go (literally and figuratively). I meditate in scriptures and become what I am meditating in. Here are just a few scriptural references:

- God gave you, man, dominion – Genesis 1:26
- Jesus was in a boat on the water (asleep, by the way) and He rebuked the storm. He arose and rebuked the wind and spoke to the sea and there was calm – Mark 4:38-39 (AMP)
- Jesus told us that we would do the works that He did and greater works - John 14:12

- Jesus told us to speak to the mountain (obstacle, problem) – Mark 11:22-24
- Greater is He that is in you, than he that is in the world – 1 John 4:4
- The same spirit that raised Jesus from the dead dwells in you. Be God inside-minded – Romans 8:11
- A thousand shall fall at your side - no evil will befall you – Psalm 91:7-10

You are a Whosoever and Seated with Christ – To Do Greater Works

At anytime and anywhere – the Word of God will work for you as a whosoever (Mark 11). Work that Word – the Word works when you work it. So, whenever you think that there is potential for a storm or turbulent weather, even slight, or even if predicted miles away from you, work the Word and keep the storms away from you, your family, your property and your community. As a believer, you are to be a doer of the Word of God – read your bible and do what it says (as Harold Herring from the Debt Free Army suggests). Practice on the weather when rain is predicted.

Through the years, I have heard many people say that they ask God to hold back the rain until they reach their homes, etc. I believe that God is a God of Grace and Mercy and Goodness and I believe that He honors that request but there is

16

what I believe to be a better way. The way is to do it the way Jesus did it – by speaking to the storms - we are to do what He did and more. Walk in all of the light that you have now in this area. God is good all of the time and I believe that He honors those heart desires and requests but wants His children to take authority.

Jesus told us that "these works and greater" would we do. Speaking to the weather and using your authority is a work that He did. And, according to Mark 11:20-24, Jesus didn't tell you to speak about the mountain - He said to speak to it. He spoke to the fig tree and not about it. He spoke to it and said the results He intended. After He spoke to the fig tree, notice that He did not turn to see if it obeyed. He did not have to check to see how the chips would fall so to speak.

If you say, "Oh, dear, look at this nasty weather and we could lose our house. So what are we going to do now?" That is speaking **about** the weather when you have been given authority **over it**. That is speaking about the mountain instead of speaking to it. You want to speak to the weather (say, pray) and then believe that it is a done deal. Because you believe that it is "done," you will want to speak the answer instead of the problem.

What Jesus Did During a Storm

What did Jesus do when there was a storm at sea? That was a demonic weather pattern – a good example for us – He was asleep on a pillow (asleep during a storm) and that is what we need to do - be asleep during a storm! Jesus got up only when the fearful disciples came and woke Him. He got up and rebuked it, spoke to it, and there was immediate peace and calm. Yes, you can peace in the midst of any storm or impending storm – speak to it and go to sleep! There have been times when people have told me about a storm from the night before and it did not even wake me because I was asleep on a pillow while the storm raged in other areas of the city. I had prayed and went to sleep without further thought and care. I had rolled the care over onto the Lord.

Steps to Tame the Weather

Sound impossible that you can have dominion over the weather? With God all things are possible. It doesn't even matter how big or turbulent the storm or how ominous the weather is. Jesus rebuked the storm and the waves **were immediately** quiet and calm. You can do it, too. Have confidence and just do it:

- Meditate in the Word of God focusing on your authority and how Jesus did it

- Pray/rebuke the storm (cover your family and property with the Blood); speak to it
- Receive it "done"
- Just believe – do not try to figure it out or reason about it
- Do not speak against your prayer (i.e., do not talk about how bad the storm looks)
- Thank and praise God

A Bad Weather Report

If you hear a report or "know" that there is a storm "brewing," and one that could possibly come near you, by all means, do what you need to take shelter, etc., in the natural.

You do not need to be caught off guard no matter where you are and how far away from your property you might be when a storm is approaching. There is power in the Name of Jesus wherever you are. Here is one prayer (just an example) if you are away from home and there is a storm approaching your home:

> Father in the Name of Jesus…. I take authority over the storm that is threatening to bring destruction to my home and family - and I loose the angels of God….. angels manifest yourselves 10, 12, 15 feet tall and protect my (homes, properties, and business) from any

spiritual or physical intruders, against any storms that would even think to come near my family or properties. I plead the Blood of Jesus over my life, home, family and possessions and speak to any storm that is in the area of (name the vicinity) and command it to go and be cast into the sea where it won't hurt anyone in the Name of Jesus... according to Mark 11, I speak to that mountain, that storm, and it obeys me. Storm, you go now, in the Name of Jesus!

Speak in Line with What You Pray

Once you speak or say or pray and believe that it is done, resist the urge to speak (or even think) anything contrary to what you just spoke (or prayed). Inevitably someone will mention how the weather "is supposed to be really bad today" just as soon as I have spoken to the storm or weather system to tell it what it needs to do. When something like that happens, I typically say nothing to them but all the while "praying in my head" but I also sometimes say something like, "Oh, it is clearing up... it is moving away from here even as we speak."

Weather Prayer Examples

Father, in the Name of Jesus, I thank you that your Word promises me divine protection and You are a very present help in time of trouble. God, you are a supernatural God... My eyes are not on myself but on You. You said that a thousand will fall by my side and ten thousand at my right but it would not come near me (Psalm 91). I thank you for your Word that promises that no evil will befall me neither shall any plague come near my dwelling (Psalm 91). I thank you that just as Jesus spoke to the storms of life, I, too, have authority over them as a child of the Most High. And, because You love me, You will protect me. I do now take my authority over this storm that is threatening to come near me and my dwelling and my family. I will not worry …I believe Your Word and I am a doer and not just a hearer of Your Word. I know that the weather must obey me since I have dominion over this earth. I plead the Blood of Jesus over my life, home, possessions and my entire family and all of our loved ones. I thank you, Father, that my family and I dwell in the secret place of the Most High God under the shadow of the Almighty. I thank You that the Blood of Jesus surrounds me, my family and property. I draw a Bloodline of Jesus around my family, my property and this neighborhood and complex that Satan cannot cross. I plead the Blood of Jesus…Storm, you go, in the Name of Jesus….Father, I know that I have divine protection this day and every day and thank you in the matchless and majestic Name of Jesus. Amen!

In the Name of Jesus, I rebuke you storm I cast you into the sea where you won't hurt anyone. You go from here. The Blood of Jesus against you... Go in the Name of Jesus!

Walking Your Property

There have been times when I have walked my property (even my apartment building) while praying and drawing a bloodline around my home and my neighbors' homes. I do that as led by the Holy Spirit and so I recommend that whatever He tells you to do – do it. I speak the words out loud... while drawing a spiritual line. The line may "look" invisible but it is a supernatural, a spiritual line. I use the words of my mouth to establish my authority on this earth and in my territory. For example, I say something like this... "I draw a Bloodline of Jesus around this property that Satan cannot cross. "

Praying for Weather Outside of Your Locale/Territory

There is no distance in the spirit - I have prayed for other "territories" and have watched the results. However, I do believe that it is under the authority of those living there to do that. I do pray for them but they need to do so as well.

One time I watched the television weather report change as a storm went back and forth along a certain line where I was praying and it looked as though perhaps those in the other state were praying and we were almost praying the storm away from us and toward them and they were praying the storm away from them and towards our locale! It went on for several hours into the next day and it was almost funny to watch.

Intentionally Speaking the Word of God Each Day

If you currently speak the Word of God over your life and circumstances, you may already be speaking the words of authority and protection; if not, then you must consider adding some "confessions" to your daily prayer and Word-of-God life. It is essential and also it is honoring God and putting Him first and foremost because it is doing His will. It is His will for all of His children to walk as Jesus walked. And, that includes speaking the Word. That is an integral part of the operation of the Kingdom of God system.

I pray for protection each day by confessing out of **Psalm 91**. Daily, I plead the Blood of Jesus over myself, possessions, my home, family all over this world, and my loved ones.

If this is somewhat new to you, you can start with a few examples of simple scripture-based confessions such as but not limited to:

I have the life and nature of God in my spirit and can do what Jesus did and greater.

No evil will befall me or my family neither shall any plague come near our dwelling.

All things are possible to me because I believe.

I speak to storms just as Jesus did and they must obey.

I have authority because God has given it to me. Therefore, I take authority and rule and reign as a king in life through Jesus (the Anointed One and His anointing).

Speaking to Tornadoes, Hurricanes, Wind and Rain

Just yesterday, there were heavy storms headed towards my home as I sat at my computer working on this book, and I took authority over those storms. The next day, it was as if no storm came into this vicinity; I had prayed them away. God is so good, isn't He? However, there were reports of trees downed and heavy rains and wind in other parts of the metro Atlanta area. It rained here at my house a little for a few minutes, and the skies were somewhat darkened, and were looking threatening, but other than that, there was no storm here. (I have learned not to pray all the rain away so we will not have drought conditions here). The storms "toppled trees and ripped down power lines in other parts of the state of Georgia." There have been many times when this happened; but, after praying, the storm did not come near me or my property. I only read about it or heard about it after the storm had passed over my dwelling place and me.

One of the most profound (almost funny) experiences that I have had with the weather was when there was a major storm predicted for Atlanta, Georgia, and its environs. This was at a time when I first started talking to the weather and commanding it to obey and "go." I was watching a television broadcast when the local weather report came on interrupting the broadcast. The weather man stood talking about the big storm coming – the turbulent weather - and I noticed that it was heading for the exact location where I lived at that time. He did the things with the radar and showed on the map what he knew to show. I immediately prayed for the storm to go and change direction and go away and immediately after I prayed the prayer, the weather man, in amazement said he had "never seen anything like this" before. He proceeded to tell the viewers that the storm had suddenly shifted direction while he was giving the storm

26

report! He turned and displayed the radar tracking the storm as proof that the storm had changed direction while he was speaking!

A few years ago, Georgia was suffering from extreme dry conditions and the state desperately needed rain and soon. Once, the governor of Georgia called for prayer and the rains came and the drought conditions subsided. I was one of those "pray-ers." Across this nation farmers prayed for rain and even the journalists had to write about it after witnessing the rains that came first hand while on assignment.

There have been so many instances where I was out walking from the train station or heading out for the day when there was threatening weather or just a heavy rain predicted. Sometimes the sky would remain dark and cloudy but the rains did not come near me after I prayed them away from me.

More Prayer Examples

You can go and draw a Blood line around your home and trees when threatening storms are approaching and pray:

In the name of Jesus, I draw a Bloodline of Jesus around my life, my home, my family and my property that Satan cannot cross. Satan, you see the Blood... you have to go in the Name of Jesus. I have authority over you. Now, go…. Thank you Jesus!

~~~

In the name of Jesus, I speak to this storm….storm, I am talking to you… you foul weather spirit. I cast you into the sea where you won't hurt anyone. I rebuke you foul weather spirit in the Name of Jesus… Go… Go from my city, from this neighborhood… Git! Praise You Father! Thank you Jesus!

~~~

Storm, go back where you came in the Name of Jesus. The Blood of Jesus against you. Go, in the Name of Jesus.

~~~

In the case of a storm that looks as though it didn't hear you (by the way, if it's on this earth, it can hear you… it has "ears"): Storm, in the Name of Jesus…. I guess you must not have heard me the first time…. Go, in the Name of Jesus! The Blood of Jesus against you…. You see the Blood, Go! Praise You Father!

Ready and Armed with the Word

So, maybe you feel as if you are not quite ready to make the sun stand still yet, but what about saving that one for the next time you are talking with someone and they mention the weather? Maybe you are confident that the sun will stand still when you tell it to... go ahead... talk to it and make some changes in the weather. Have confidence in God...after all, it's not your ability that will change the weather, it is His.

Prayer for Salvation (To become a child of God)

Father in the Name of Jesus, I come to you. I know that I am a sinner. I believe that you sent Your son, Jesus, to die on the cross for my sins. I thank you for forgiveness of my sins. I believe that you raised Jesus from the dead. I now confess Jesus as Lord of my life. Come into my life and do something awesome with it. I thank you Father that I am saved and that I am now part of the household of God, Your beloved child.

Resources and Additional Information to Help Grow Your Faith

Here are some related resources including other recommended reading and websites:

My website: www.ilenesaidel.com

www.worldchangers.org

www.KCM.org

The Believer's Authority by Kenneth E. Hagin

The Authority of the Believer by John A. MacMillan

Faith Food Devotions by Kenneth E. Hagin

The Blood and the Glory by Billye Brim

John G. Lake: His Life, His Sermons, His Boldness of Faith by Kenneth Copeland

The Tongue: A Creative Force by Charles Capps

God's Creative Power Gift Collection by Charles Capps

For more information, please contact:

Ilene Saidel - P.O. Box 76873, Atlanta, GA 30358
404-865-1497

Made in the USA
Lexington, KY
07 May 2016